AMAZING
SCIENCE

W9-AVC-217

PULL, LIFT, AND LOWER

A Book About Pulleys

by Michael Dahl
illustrated by Denise Shea

Special thanks to our advisers for their expertise:

Youwen Xu, Professor
Department of Physics and Astronomy
Minnesota State University, Mankato, Minn.

Susan Kesselring, M.A.
Literacy Educator
Rosemount–Apple Valley–Eagan (Minnesota) School District

PICTURE WINDOW BOOKS
Minneapolis, Minnesota

A PULLEY IS A MACHINE

A pulley is a simple machine. A simple machine is anything that helps people do work. Work can mean lifting heavy loads or moving things up and down.

A pulley uses a wheel and a rope, or cable. The rope wraps over the wheel. When the rope is pulled at one end, the wheel helps lift the rope

FLAGPOLES

Outside the school building, a flag is attached to a long rope. When one end of the rope is pulled down, the other end lifts the flag to the top of the tall pole. The flagpole uses a pulley to raise the flag to the top, where it flutters and flaps in the wind.

MOVING HEAVY SAILS

Block and tackle is used to hoist, or lift, heavy sails on a sailboat. The ropes that lift and lower sails are called halyards. Using a block and tackle, one person can lift a sail that weighs twice as much as a grown adult.

FIRST-CLASS PULLEY

A first-class pulley uses a wheel that stays in one place. The pulley's rope moves up and down, and the wheel turns around a point called the axle. The axle on a first-class pulley never moves. It helps keep the wheel steady.

A first-class pulley helps people pull a bucket of water up a deep well. People all over the world use this type of pulley.

TO LEARN MORE

MORE BOOKS TO READ

Douglas, Lloyd G. *What Is a Pulley?* New York: Children's Press, 2002.

Fowler, Allan. *Simple Machines.* New York: Children's Press, 2001.

Frost, Helen & Gail Saunders-Smith. *What Are Pulleys.* Mankato, Minn.: Pebble Books, 2001.

Walker, Sally M & Roseann Feldmann. Minneapolis, Minn.: *Pulleys.* Lerner, 2001.

INDEX

blinds, 8

cable, 4, 7, 17, 23

flagpole, 10, 23

halyards, 14

pulley, 4, 6, 7, 8, 10, 12, 17, 18, 20, 22, 23

wheel, 7, 8, 12, 17, 18, 23

ON THE WEB

FactHound offers a safe, fun way to find Internet sites related to this book. All of the sites on FactHound have been researched by our staff.

1. Visit *www.facthound.com*

2. Type in this special code for age-appropriate sites: *1404813055*

3. Click on the FETCH IT button. Your trusty FactHound will fetch the best sites for you!

LOOK FOR ALL OF THE BOOKS IN THE AMAZING SCIENCE SERIES:

Air: Outside, Inside, and All Around	1-4048-0248-7	Pull, Lift, and Lower: A Book About Pulleys	1-4048-1305-5
Cut, Chop, and Stop: A Book About Wedges	1-4048-1307-1	Rocks: Hard, Soft, Smooth, and Rough	1-4048-0015-8
Dirt: The Scoop on Soil	1-4048-0012-3	Roll, Slope, and Slide: A Book About Ramps	1-4048-1304-7
Electricity: Bulbs, Batteries, and Sparks	1-4048-0245-2	Scoop, Seesaw, and Raise: A Book About Levers	1-4048-1303-9
Energy: Heat, Light, and Fuel	1-4048-0249-5	Sound: Loud, Soft, High, and Low	1-4048-0016-6
Light: Shadows, Mirrors, and Rainbows	1-4048-0013-1	Temperature: Heating Up and Cooling Down	1-4048-0247-9
Magnets: Pulling Together, Pushing Apart	1-4048-0014-X	Tires, Spokes, and Sprockets: A Book About Wheels	1-4048-1308-X
Matter: See It, Tough It, Taste It, Smell It	1-4048-0246-0	Twist, Dig, and Drill: A Book About Screws	1-4048-1306-3
Motion: Push and Pull, Fast and Slow	1-4048-0250-9	Water: Up, Down, and All Around	14048-0017-4a